You are never too young or old to do something new. All my life I have loved to write stories and poems. I have never before had a book published. Now that I am old (great-grandma old), my dreams have come true. So never give up hoping and dreaming, because it is never too late.

Irene Bartlett

With Best Wishes

Irene Bartlett

The New Testament
Bible Poems for Children

THE NEW TESTAMENT
Bible Poems for Children

Irene Bartlett

ATHENA PRESS
LONDON

The New Testament
Bible Poems for Children
Copyright © Irene Bartlett 2007

All Rights Reserved

No part of this book may be reproduced in any form
by photocopying or by any electronic or mechanical means,
including information storage or retrieval systems,
without permission in writing from both the copyright
owner and the publisher of this book.

ISBN 10-digit: 1 84748 207 4
ISBN 13-digit: 978 1 84748 207 5

First Published 2007 by
ATHENA PRESS
Queen's House, 2 Holly Road
Twickenham TW1 4EG
United Kingdom

Printed for Athena Press

Note from the Author

This book of stories from the Bible, told in verse, is suitable for children to hear and understand at a very young age. Hopefully, they will want to return to it over and over again as they grow older, and then in turn read it to their own children.

These poems are intended to be read aloud to children by their parents, grandparents and teachers. When children are old enough to read, they should be encouraged to read them aloud themselves. They will become familiar with verse and grow to love it, as I did, and as my children did when they were young.

My thanks go to:

Angela Flexen, for spending many hours of her time doing the black and white drawings that illustrate each story, and for her encouragement and guidance.

To all my friends for their encouragement.

To my family, who believed that I could achieve my dreams.

To the staff and children from Victoria Road Infant School in Cirencester, who inspired me and who rejoiced in my success.

Mainly, my thanks go to God and the Holy Spirit, for inspiring me to write these poems, and for giving me the talent to do so.

I dedicate this work to my daughter, Jane (the miracle that God worked for me); to my son, Christopher; and to the memory of my late husband, Chris.

Contents

The Christmas Story	11
The Boy in the Temple	15
John the Baptist	19
Jesus Chooses his Friends	23
Water into Wine	25
Down through the Roof	29
Storm on the Lake	31
Jairus' Daughter	35
Feeding of the Multitude	37
The Good Neighbour	41
Mary and Martha	43
Healing the Blind	47
The Foolish Builders	49
The Rich Man's Party	53
The Lost Sheep	55
The Lost Coin	59
Getting into Heaven	62
The Prodigal Son	64
The Tenth Leper	68
Jesus and the Children	72
Zacchaeus the Taxman	74
The Happy Parade	78

The Important Meal	80
The Saddest Day	84
The Happiest Day	86
I Don't Believe It	90
The Final Goodbye	92

The Christmas Story

Once upon a time, in a place called Nazareth town –
Not a place of any particular renown –
A young girl called Mary lived with her father and mother.
She was engaged to Joseph, and they loved one another.

Joseph was a carpenter who was good and kind,
He was one of the gentlest men you ever could find.
Mary was a good and obedient daughter,
And listened carefully to the things her mother taught her.

One day an angel appeared to Mary.
My goodness! That must have been very scary.
'Fear not,' said the angel, 'God's message I bring,
For you have been chosen to do a wonderful thing.

'You are to have a baby boy
Who will bring you and Joseph so much joy.
This boy you must call Jesus, meaning 'holy one'.
He is very special; he is God's son.'

Mary thought she must be special to God, and very blessed,
Though not for one moment could she have guessed
Why he had chosen her to be mother to his son,
But she accepted God's will, and said, 'Let it be done.'

The angel came to Joseph in a dream,
And he told him the same news, and Jesus' name.
So Joseph and Mary married and prepared for the event.
When Jesus would be born, God's son would be sent.

Then Joseph received some very bad news.
They had to go to Bethlehem to pay their dues.
So on a donkey Mary was mounted,
And they set off on the journey to be counted.

When they arrived in Bethlehem, they couldn't find a bed,
But they were offered a stable instead.
It wasn't what they wanted, but what could they say?
At least it was warm and dry; and the baby was on the way!

It was here, on this very first Christmas night,
That Jesus was born, in the lantern light.
With only the donkey and cows to witness the scene,
Lay Mary with Joseph, and the baby between.

They both thanked God, and said a prayer,
And Mary laid Jesus in a manger there.
Then Joseph and Mary lay down to sleep,
And the animals stood by, their watch to keep.

Then, during the night, there was a tap on the door,
And there stood shepherds – twenty or more.
An angel had told them that Jesus was born,
And had sent a star to guide them just before dawn.

They brought lambs to give to God's son,
And they knelt and thanked God for what he had done.
Later they were visited by three wise men of old,
Who had been watching and waiting for what had been foretold.

They too brought gifts for the infant baby,
Gifts he would need during his lifetime, maybe,
Gifts of frankincense, myrrh, and gold,
Each with a meaning; as they had foretold
That a baby would come into the world one day,
Who would grow up a man, who would show the way
For man to live as God wanted him to:
With kindness and love his whole life through.

Through him, evil would be overcome,
And God's will would always be done.
And sins would be forgiven,
So that all at last would go to heaven.

The Boy in the Temple

The baby was born in Bethlehem, in Nazareth he grew;
Mary, his mother, taught him all that she knew.
Joseph, his earthly father, showed him how to carve with wood,
And he obeyed both his parents, for he was very good.

He did all the things that little boys did:
He worked and played, and did as he was bid.
Then, when he was twelve, a special treat was planned:
A trip to Jerusalem, the Holy Land.

It was a trip to the temple for the Passover,
And Jesus went with his father and mother.
It had been such a wonderful day to celebrate,
And they started back when it was quite late.

All the families journeyed together
Under the stars in the fine weather.
They rested and had meals while the children played.
Then they sang psalms, and together they prayed.

Mary and Joseph didn't worry that Jesus did not stay with them,
For they knew most of the families that travelled with them.
The children ran back and forth between each family,
And could come to no harm, they just played happily.

It wasn't until early next morning,
Just as the sun came up and the day was dawning,
That Mary went in search of Jesus to come and break bread,
But she came back to Joseph crying instead.

'I cannot find him,' Mary cried aloud,
'I've looked everywhere in the crowd.
I have asked everyone and they have not seen him.
What shall we do? I fear we have lost him.'

'We will have to go back,' Joseph said.
So they turned around to return to Jerusalem instead.
And they asked everyone they met along the way
If they had seen a young boy on his own that day.

But everyone just shook their heads and said, 'Sorry, no.'
And went on walking where they had to go.
At last they reached Jerusalem, and they saw one of the preachers,
He was one of the temple teachers.

Again, they asked if he had seen their young boy,
And the preacher's eyes lit up with joy.
'I know where that son of yours is, just go back to the temple.
He is there, talking and listening with the people.

'He is asking all kinds of questions, far beyond his years.'
And the preacher's eyes filled with tears.
'The priests are amazed at what he is saying.
And the people all around are praying.'

When Mary and Joseph reached the temple, they watched for a while.
Then Mary took Jesus' hand, and said with a smile,
'Come along, my son, that will be enough for today.
We have travelled and worried for a very long way.'

Jesus obeyed, and travelled home, and said that he was sad.
He had not meant to worry them, but he was glad
He had been able to spend time in the house of his heavenly father,
Though he said he would always love his earthly father and mother.

And Mary and Joseph understood:
Their son was very kind and good.
But soon he would be grown, and would have work to do.
What it was, only God knew.

John the Baptist

When Jesus grew to be a man, he set out happily
To visit John, who was of Mary's family.
God had given John a job, a very special one.
It was to prepare the way for Jesus, God's son.

John preached to the people by the River Jordan,
And it was here that he baptised them.
He said, 'God is sending someone very special to you,
And I am not worthy to tie his shoe.'

Some people thought John was quite mad.
He wore an old hairy shirt, and for dinner, locusts he had.
But as he preached to them one day,
He overheard a man in the crowd say,

'You don't think this man is the chosen one, do you?'
And the other man said, 'I was wondering that too.'
And John called out, 'No! I am not he,
But he is coming, so don't you see?
'You must repent of your sins now, while there is still time,
And be baptised, just as I am.'

Then Jesus arrived, and came up to John,
'I want you to baptise me too, just as you have done
To all my people. You have washed their sins away.
So please, will you baptise me too on this wonderful day?'

John was amazed, and he knelt before him,
'How can I baptise you, when you are without sin?'
'God wants it this way,' Jesus replied.
'For my work here must now start,' he said with a sigh.

And so side by side they went into the river,
His son, John asked God to deliver.
And as Jesus rose from the water, a dove flew from above,
And God's voice was heard to say, 'This is my son, whom I love.'

Jesus Chooses his Friends

Jesus grew up in Galilee,
And when he reached the age of thirty,
He started the work that God wanted him to do.
He told stories to the people, as we do to you.

He told of God's kingdom in Heaven above;
He told them of his father's love.
He taught them to love one another;
To treat everyone as though he were their brother.

One day, when he had taught for a long time by the lake,
He was tired and thought he would like to take a break.
So he called to some fishermen out in the sea,
'May I come into your boat? Will you row it for me?'

'Of course,' said Andrew, one of the fishermen,
And he rowed back to shore there and then.
'We are wasting our time fishing, we haven't caught a thing.
Perhaps some luck to us, you will bring.'

And Jesus told them just where to row to,
Where to lower their nets, and what to do.
Suddenly there were swarms of fish swimming around,
The splashing in the water making a great sound.

And soon the fishermen's nets were full,
And to get them into the boats took a lot of pull.
Other fishermen passing by looked up, and heard Andrew shout.
They came to see what the fuss was about.

They had never seen so many fish – soon all boats were full.
And back to the shore they went with their haul.
Then Andrew said in a very loud voice,
'Come, let us thank God and rejoice.

'For only he could have helped us like that,'
And they all sat together on a rush mat.
And Jesus told them about his heavenly father,
And Andrew introduced him to Peter, his brother.

Jesus said, 'I need some helpers with the work I must do,
I think my father has chosen you.
Will you leave your fishing boats and come with me?
Will you leave your home and family?

'Will you be with me until my work here is done?'
And there, beneath the evening sun,
They promised they would go with him, wherever he went,
And help to do God's work, wherever they were sent.

Water into Wine

A wedding was taking place, and Mary and Jesus were invited.
It was a wonderful day, and everyone was excited.
The bride and groom looked so happy,
As together they stood, under the canopy.

Everything was going fine
When the guests sat down to dine.
The food and wine tasted very good,
And everyone was in a cheerful mood.

Then Mary overheard some servants say,
'How are we going to tell our host what has happened today?
All the wine is gone, not a drop is left.
Everyone will be bereft.'

Mary spoke to the servants and told them what to do,
'My son Jesus will help; just do what he tells you.'
Then she told Jesus what she had done,
'I know you can help them, my dear son.'

Jesus looked at his mother and replied,
'My work has not yet started,' then he sighed,
'But because you have asked me to do this thing,
Go tell the servants that they must bring
Vats full of water, drawn from the well.
And I will pray, and who can tell?
My father in heaven will know what to do.
He will work a miracle for you.'

The servants did as they were told
And brought the water, sparkling and cold.
'Now,' said Jesus, 'pour some into a cup,
And take it to the host and let him drink it up.'

Again, the servants did as they were told,
And were shocked and amazed, for, lo and behold,
When the host tasted the water, it had turned to wine.
Wine that was wonderful, really fine.

The guests all remarked that in the past,
The cheapest wine was always served last.
But on this very special day, something strange had been seen,
And the servants knew that Jesus had asked God to intervene.

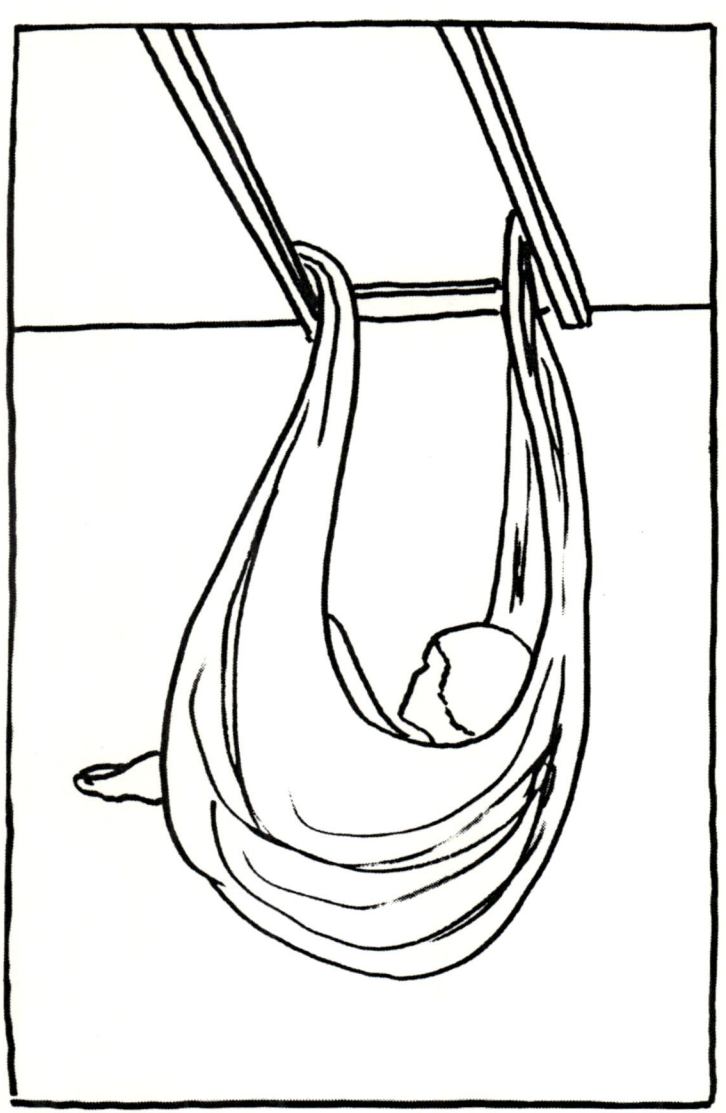

Down through the Roof

Jesus was invited into a friend's house to preach,
And lots of people wanted to know what he would teach.
Everyone pushed and shoved to get in,
Tall folk, short folk, fat and thin.

Soon there was not a space to be found,
And outside a man lay on the ground.
His friends had carried him, for he couldn't walk,
And he had so much wanted to hear Jesus talk.

He had heard that Jesus could cure the lame,
The sick, the blind, and even the insane.
But now, as he lay on the ground in the dust,
He had to find a way to see Jesus, he knew he must.

Then he turned to his friends and said,
'Do you think that you can carry my bed?
If you can lift me up onto the roof, which is flat,
You could lower me through the ceiling on a mat.'

His friends set about doing as he asked,
And they managed to carry out the task.
Making a hole that was big and wide,
They lowered him down to the room inside.

They set him down beside Jesus, gently,
Who smiled and looked at him softly,
'All your sins of the past, I forgive,' he said,
As he laid his hands on the man's head.

'Wait a minute,' shouted his friend, angrily.
'Only God can do that, surely.'
'That is so,' Jesus replied, 'but is it not the same
To forgive a man's sins or cure the lame!'

'And to prove to you that God works through me,
I will cure this lame man so that you can see
That curing his body or curing his soul
Is to make him better, to make him whole.'

And turning to the lame man, he said,
'My son, get up off your bed.'
And the man rose up, and walked without pain,
And vowed that he would not sin again.

Storm on the Lake

Jesus and his twelve friends were out fishing,
And the boat was gently swaying.
The sun above was very warm,
And the sea below was very calm.

Jesus closed his eyes and drifted off to sleep,
While his friends rowed off into the deep.
Then a dark, black cloud filled the sky,
And the wind blew the waves up very high.

The boat began tossing;
The wind was howling.
The men were shouting in fear,
'Let us row hard back to the shore, we must get out
  of here.'

But the waves were too rough, soaring up high,
And the men were afraid that they were going to
  die.
Still, Jesus was fast asleep, relaxed and resting;
Unaware of what was happening.

Peter shook him, shouting, 'Please help us.
We are all going to drown Jesus,
While you are lying down sleeping.
The storm is getting worse and raging.'

Jesus awoke, and standing, raised his arm,
And instantly the sea was calm.
The clouds parted, and way up high,
The sun was shining in a clear blue sky.

Then Jesus turned to his friends and said,
'Why were you afraid, you should have had faith instead.
My father in heaven would not have let us drown,
He would never let us down.'

So, once again, Jesus had worked a miracle for his friends to see.
To prove he was God's son, by controlling the sea.
And the winds and waves had obeyed his will.
Amazing them then and inspiring us still.

Jairus' Daughter

Jairus had a daughter, whom he loved dearly,
And that she loved her father could be seen clearly.
They were a happy, loving family,
Always laughing and singing happily.
Then one day the daughter became sick.
It had happened suddenly, oh so quick.

They sent for the doctor, who stood by her bed,
Then he looked at Jairus sadly and shook his head.
'This illness, to me, is really quite new,
I just don't know what I can do.
All I can suggest is that you pray,
And go and find Jesus who is not far away.'

So Jairus went in search of Jesus, who was preaching to a crowd,
And he called to him in a voice very loud.
'Jesus I need you to come and cure my child.
She is a good girl, obedient, meek and mild.
'I know you can make her well, so come quickly please,'
Jairus begged down on his knees.

Jesus bent down and pulled him to his feet,
'Come, my friend, your daughter I must meet'.
But as they began walking away, Jesus stopped still.
Someone else was very ill.
A woman who had been sick for many years
Was standing behind him in tears.

'You touched my gown,' Jesus said to her.
'Yes,' said the woman, 'I wanted a cure.
I did not want to disturb you, as you were busy.
I just reached out my hand because I felt dizzy.'
'Because you believe I can make you well –
And I know you believe, I can tell –
Your illness is no longer with you, it is gone.'
And he took Jairus' arm, and they hurried along.

But as they came near to Jairus' home,
They heard someone cry and moan.
A servant came to meet them and said,
'Master, it is too late, the poor child is dead.'
Jairus wept and fell to the ground,
And everyone watched without a sound.
Then Jesus looked up to heaven, whispered a prayer,
And turned to those standing there.

'Don't worry, you can stop your weeping,
For the child is only sleeping.'
'Oh no,' said the servant, 'she is dead.
I saw her for myself as she lay on her bed.'
Jesus went into the house taking Peter, James and John,
And they were not gone for very long.
Jesus took the dead girl's cold hand,
And in a soft voice gave a command.

'Wake up, little girl,' Jesus said,
And she stirred and then sat up in bed.
Her eyes became bright, and her face started glowing,
And she jumped out of bed and hugged Jesus knowing
Something wonderful had happened, a miracle had taken place,
And her father hugged her with a smile on his face.
'Dear father, I am hungry,' the little girl said.
So instead of a wake they had a feast instead.

Feeding of the Multitude

Jesus preached to the crowds each day,
But did they listen to what he had to say?
Did they heed him, was he heard?
Did they pass on his every word?

He taught that it was wicked to deceive,
And more blessed to give than to receive.
To steal from each other was a sin,
And to temptation they should not give in.
They should love one another:
Father, mother, sister and brother.
He taught them who their neighbour was,
And that they should love them because,
'Just as my father loves me, so I love you,
And this is what I want you to do:
If a man has two coats to keep him warm,
While another only has one that is old and torn,
Then give him one coat, you cannot wear two,
And you show him God's love if this you do.'

As the crowds gathered to hear what he had to say,
On that very hot and sticky day,
Jesus said to his friends, 'They are tired and need
  something to eat.
They have come a long way in this heat.'
A small boy standing by heard what was said,
And he offered up some fish and some bread.
'It isn't much I know, and it will not go far,
But you may have it, here you are.'

Jesus smiled at the little boy,
And his heart filled with joy.
The people today would witness
The power of God and his kindness.

'Find me some baskets,' he said.
And in each he placed a small piece of fish and some bread.
'Pass them out to the people and let them see,
The wonders that God performs through me.'

And so the baskets went from father to mother,
To friend, and enemy, to sister and brother.
Everyone took food, and they all were fed,
And a miracle was worked, in the breaking of bread.

And when they had all had their fill,
Seven baskets were collected, and there was bread in them still.
The people were astounded at what they saw,
Jesus had worked a miracle once more.

He told them his father in heaven loved each and every one,
And that he was his beloved son,
That the food they had eaten was a gift to them,
And they praised his name, and said 'Amen'.

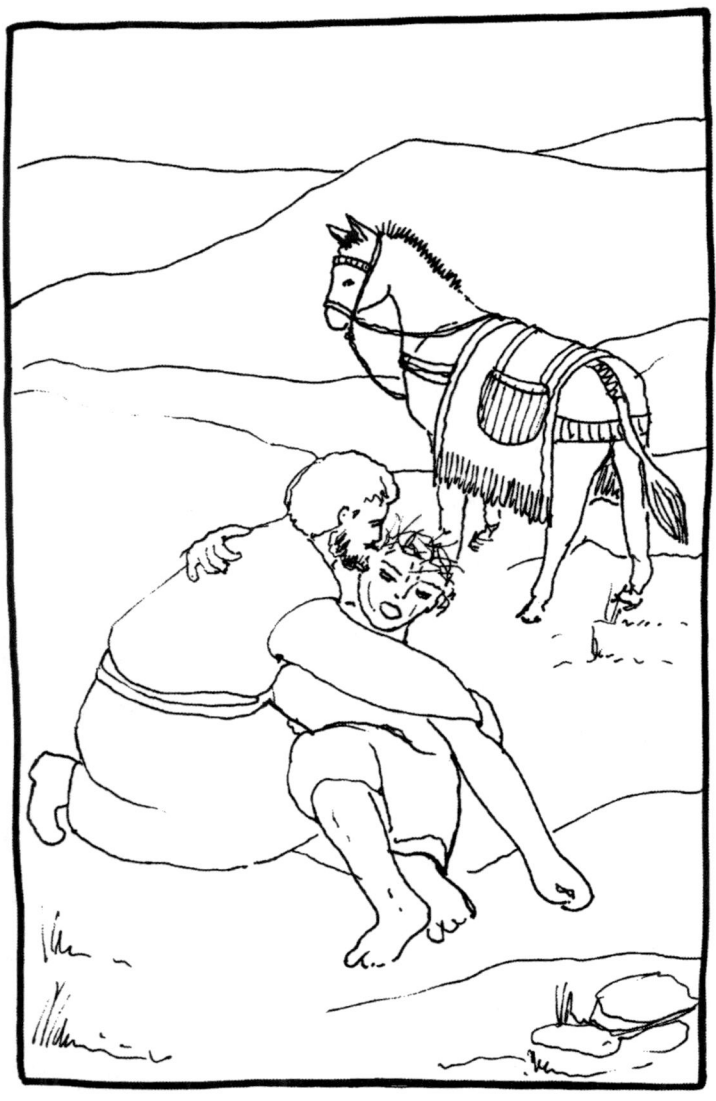

The Good Neighbour

Jesus spoke to the people all around,
And the people listened; there was not a sound.
He told them to love their neighbours,
And to help them with their labours.

'Tend them when they are sick and lame,
Then, for you, they will do the same.
Feed them and care for them if they are poor;
Never turn them away if they come to your door.'

Then, one man listening in the crowd
Turned to Jesus and called out loud,
'Who is my neighbour? I want to know.
Perhaps you can tell us before you go?'

'I will ask you who your neighbour is,'
Said Jesus, 'when you have heard one of my stories.'
And the people all sat down on the ground,
And Jesus smiled as he looked around.

'Once upon a time, a man was travelling along a road.
He carried a bag on his back: a heavy load.
Some robbers were waiting in hiding for him,
They attacked him and beat him and took everything.
They left him bleeding and almost dead by the side of the road.
Then off they went, carrying their heavy load.

A little while later, a priest came by.
He saw the man and he gave a sigh.
But he did not stop; instead he covered his face,
And hurried by at a very quick pace.
Another man on his way to the temple to pray
Saw the man lying there, but quickly moved away.

Then along came a Samaritan,' said Jesus, watching the crowd,
And he heard them gasp and cry aloud.
Samaritans, you see, were detested by all.
They were different and not to be trusted at all.

When the crowd quietened, Jesus went on,
'The Samaritan saw the man, and what the robbers had done.
He stopped, and lifted the man onto his donkey,
And, walking himself, he continued his journey.

When they came to an inn, he carried the man in,
And asked for a room and someone to help him.
He paid for food and a bed, till the man became better,
Now can you tell me, who was the man's neighbour?'

And a voice from the crowd answered Jesus that day:
'It was not the priest, or the man going to pray.
It was the Samaritan, who saved the poor man.
He was the good neighbour, the others just ran.'

'Now you know,' Jesus said, 'who your neighbour is.
It is everyone around you that you can assist.
And when you are in trouble, they will help you,
And they will love you as much as God does too.'

Mary and Martha

Martha was not very happy. it seemed quite unfair
That there was dust and dirt everywhere.
The floors all needed scrubbing
And the furniture needed rubbing.

There was food that needed cooking
And clothes that needed washing.
And why, she asked herself, *should I do it all,*
When Mary, my sister, does nothing at all?

Jesus had come to visit, and he and Mary were having a chat
While poor old Martha rushed around, doing this and that.
Soon they would be hungry and wanting to be fed,
And she had not yet had time to bake the bread.

Then Jesus looked up, smiled at Martha and said,
'You must not be cross with Mary for staying with me instead.
You work hard keeping everything beautifully clean.
This is one of the tidiest houses I have ever seen.

'But sometimes it is more important to spare time to chat,
About important matters, you know, this and that!
So put away your brooms and dusters, and come and sit by me,
And we will talk of God's work, and his messages from me.

'God tells us that we all have jobs in life to do,
And what is important for some may not be important to you.
We are all different and we have to find our place,
And work our way to heaven, earning God's grace.'

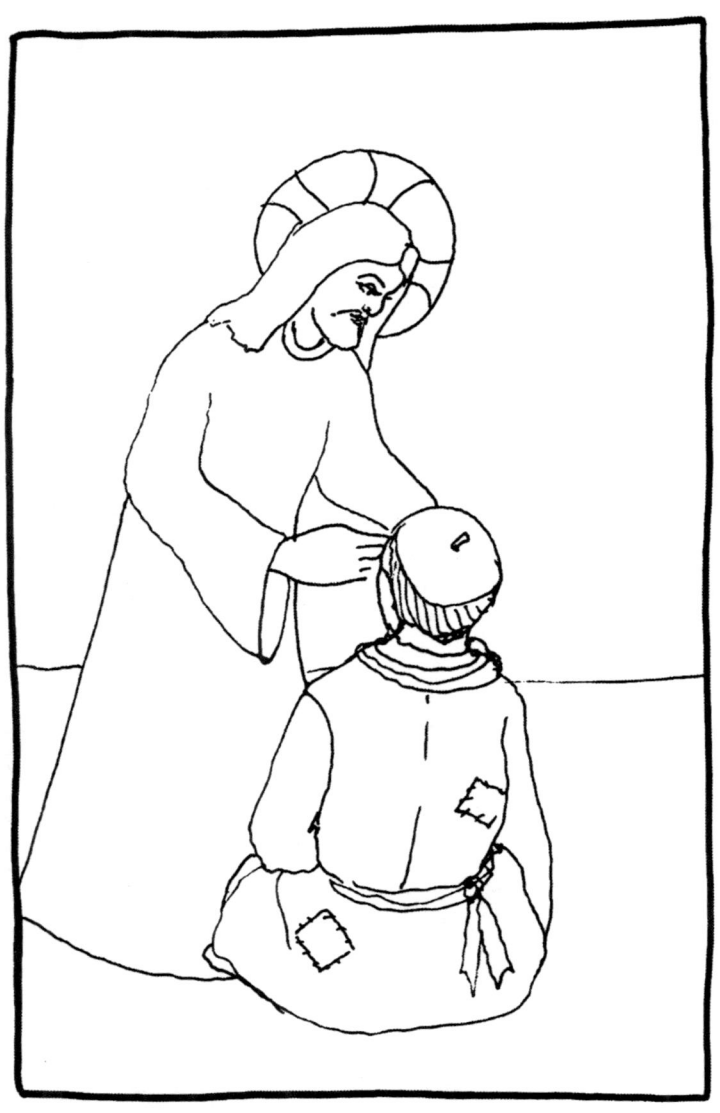

Healing the Blind

One day, when Jesus was out walking,
He and his friends were talking.
'Tell me, Jesus,' one asked, 'why is this man blind?
The answer to this question I would like to find.
Is it because his parents did something bad?
Because if it is, it makes me feel sad.'
'Oh no, of course not,' Jesus replied,
And he put his arms around the blind man and sighed.

'Come my friend, there is something I can do.
I will give back your sight to you.'
So Jesus knelt down on the ground,
And picked up some dirt that he found.
And on this he spat and made some paste,
And he rubbed it into the man's eyes and face.
'Now go,' he said, 'and wash your eyes.'
And the man could then see, much to his surprise.

The people were all amazed at what they saw,
And they cheered as they gazed at the man in awe.
Then a voice was heard from the crowd,
A man called out to Jesus very loud,
'Today is the Sabbath, and no work should be done.
Healing is work, and you healed this one.
How can you say that you are sent from God
When you break God's laws? Do you think you should?
Or maybe the man wasn't blind at all,
He was a beggar, as I recall.'

So Jesus turned to the man who had been blind and said,
'I know it is the Sabbath, so would it have been better instead
If I had left you blind, unable to see?
Or was it better to do God's work through me?'
And the man replied, with tears in his eyes,
'I may have been blind, but I didn't tell lies.'
All my life I have been blind, unable to see,
Now I have sight, God's gift to me.
And I will thank God on this Sabbath day,
That he sent Jesus to pass by my way.'

The Foolish Builders

Jesus used lots of stories to explain things to people
And each story was called a parable.
One day, while preaching to a very large crowd,
Jesus told them this story, as they sat on the ground:

'Once there was a very wise man who was going to build a house.
He didn't hurry, he thought about it carefully because
He wanted it to last for a very long time.
So he had to find a place that was good and fine.

'He came across a large rock, big and strong.
If I build here, he thought, *I'll come to no harm.*
It was very hard work, and it made his back ache,
And a very long time it seemed to take.

'But when it was done, it stood steady and firm,
And when the wind blew it came to no harm.
When the rains fell, it was built up high,
Well above the floods, up in the sky.

'Now,' said Jesus, 'there was a foolish man, with his head all hazy,
Who was somewhat idle, in fact he was lazy.
He needed a house too, so he chose some land.
It was on a beach covered in sand.

'It was easy to dig and needed no excavation.
He just built the house on the sand, with no foundation.
Soon the winds came, and blew the house awry,
And the rains came pelting down from the sky.'

'The seas rose, and the house began to sway,
And soon it was washed clean away.
So,' said Jesus, 'I want you to listen, and be like the wise man.
Listen and do everything that you can.

'To follow my way and hear what I say,
Live your life well and always pray.
For my Church will be built on a rock that is firm,
Where all those who enter will be free from harm.'

The Rich Man's Party

A rich man held a party, and he invited Jesus to attend.
Jesus went along because he was his friend.
But when the party ended, Jesus turned to him and spoke,
'You invited all the wrong people, all the wrong folk.'

'What do you mean?' asked the rich man.
'These are all my friends, every man and woman.'
'Of course,' said Jesus, 'and when they have a party too,
There is always an invitation for you.'

'What is wrong with that?' the man replied.
'I will tell you,' said Jesus and sighed.
'Next time you have a party, invite the sick and the poor.
Ask the crippled and the blind folk to come through your door.

'This will make God happy.
He will smile on you and say,
"This man has done something very kind,
And has given something away.
Instead of thinking of himself alone,
He has thought of others and a good deed has done."

'And one day God will hold a party,
And he will invite everyone to come.
Not just the rich and wealthy,
But all those who love him, each and every one.'

The Lost Sheep

The people gathered to hear what Jesus had to say.
There was always a crowd, every day.
Jesus told them stories so that they could see
How God has great love for you and me.

Now, in the hills around them were herds of sheep,
And shepherds to watch over them, their watch to keep.
So Jesus chose this subject, so the people would understand,
To show that if we stray, God is always at hand.

*Baa, baa, baa*ing,
Like babies crying.
The sheep all around,
Making the sound.

The shepherd sitting in the sun,
Knowing the sounds of every one.
Each sheep, each lamb known to him.
So he closed his eyes, and listened in.

He listened to the bleating,
The *baa baa*s repeating,
And with his mind's eye he was counting
Each number mounting.

Ninety-one, ninety-two,
Yes, that is the fluffy white ewe.
Ninety-three, ninety-four.
Nearly finished, just six more.

Ninety-seven, ninety-eight,
That is the one that got stuck in the gate.
Then the shepherd knew something was wrong,
No sound from the hundredth sheep, where had it gone?

He counted them all over again,
And still only ninety nine remain.
He would have to find the last one, he knew,
But what was he to do?

He knew it wasn't a ewe or a ram.
The one that was missing was a poor wee lamb.
It had strayed from the others and was gone.
He had to find it and save it from harm.

He herded the other sheep together in a safe place,
And he set out quickly at a very good pace.
And as he walked, he listened until he heard
The sound of a bleat: the one missing from the herd.

Then under a bush, the lamb he found,
Shaking and frightened on the ground.
The shepherd picked it up, spoke gently and soft,
And he placed it on his shoulder and carried it aloft.

And when they reached the herd,
A joyous sound was heard:
All the other sheep *baa*'d aloud, for behold!
The little lamb had returned to the fold.

Then Jesus explained to the people
About this example:
'God is the good shepherd, and he loves his sheep.
You are the sheep, and God watches even when you are asleep.

'He will always keep you safe from harm;
He will feed you and keep you warm.
And if from life's path you should stray,
He will come and find you, to show you the way.

And those who own that they have done wrong,
The angels above will welcome with a song.
For God has the power to forgive,
And in heaven, with him, they will live.

'And God knows each and every one
Over all the earth and under the sun.
And each one is precious, and he cares for all,
And he hears us when to him we call.'

The Lost Coin

Oh dear, oh dear? What can I do?
I've lost a coin, and I have so few,
I need it for my rent and my food,
And I've looked and looked but it's no good.
I've looked up the chimney, and under the stair,
I've looked and I've looked, but it isn't there.
I've looked in the larder, and under the mat,
I've even searched every inch of the cat.
I've looked in the saucepans, and even the stove,
I've searched down below, and even above.
I've thought of all the places I can look.
I've even gone through the pages in my book.
I've been out into the garden, and searched the shed.
And I've taken all the bedclothes off my bed.
I am so weary I don't know what to do,
I feel like crying, *boo-hoo, boo-hoo*.

Perhaps I should just kneel quietly by my chair,
And just have a word with God, just say a prayer.

'Dear God, help me, I don't know what to do.
Please tell me the answer, I will listen to you.
I've searched for the lost coin that I must find,
And I am nearly going out of my mind.
I'll just sit quietly, and listen to you,
And you will tell me what to do.'

Hurrah! I have found it. Oh dear, what a plight.
No wonder the coin was out of sight.
But God told me just what to do:
All I had to do was to take off my shoe!

Oh! Thank you Lord. I've been blessed this way.
I will tell all my friends about you today.
That the coin that was lost has been found,
And we will sing and we'll skip and we'll dance all around.

So if we should get lost, and our way we cannot find,
We can ask God to find us, for he is kind,
We can say we are sorry for the wrongs we have done,
And to our rescue, he will come.

Because he is loving and forgiving,
He too will be dancing and smiling,
The angels will sing, and skip all around,
For the little lost one has been found.

Getting into Heaven

As Jesus preached to the people one day,
He heard a man in the crowd say,
'Tell me how to get into heaven, Jesus.'
So Jesus told him one of his stories:

'A rich man went to the temple to pray.
He did this three times every day.
He had his own special place,
And he stood and smiled around him, raising his face.

'He was dressed in a gown of very fine wool,
And a servant fanned him to keep him cool.
A fine embroidered shawl covered his head:
The stitches sewn with a golden thread.

'Then, raising his eyes to heaven, and his voice,
He said he had come once again to rejoice.
"Lord, I am a good man, that you know,
But I will remind you before I go.

"I treat my servants well, and give alms to the poor,
I give scraps from my table to beggars at my door.
I'm sure you will remember, when at last I come to you,
How good I have been and will know what to do.
My special place in heaven will be by your side,
And I will take that place with pride."'

There was not a sound from the crowd
As Jesus smiled and looked around.
'Now I will tell you a different tale,
And there is a difference as you will tell.

'At the back of the temple, hiding behind a screen,
Stood an old woman, not wanting to be seen.
Her clothes were old and worn,
And were patched where they had been torn.

'She did not raise her eyes above.
She just thought of God, and her heart filled with love.
She thanked him for keeping her from harm,
And giving her the sun to keep her warm.

'She thanked him for friends and family.
They didn't have much but lived happily.
She knew that one day the time would come
When God would open his arms and welcome her home.'

Then Jesus said, 'Remember what I tell you.
If you want to get to heaven,
This is what you must do:
Keep God's commandments and follow me.
I am the light of the world, that lets you see.'

Those who exalt themselves will be humbled,
Only those who are humble will be exalted.
Just because a man is rich does not mean he is special.
To get into heaven, he may not be able.

Because he can afford to give to the poor,
Doesn't mean he loves them more.
Only by proving that he helps them with love,
Can he enter into heaven above.

The Prodigal Son

A father had two sons, and he loved them both the same.
But one day, the youngest to him came,
'Father, I want to ask a question, and perhaps you'll tell me:
When you die, who will get all your money?'

'My dear son, you will share my wealth with your brother.
There are just the two of you, for I have no other.'
'But,' said the boy, 'that could be a long time away,
And I would like to have my share now, today.

'I want to go travelling to foreign places,
I want to meet people of different races.'
And so, because he loved his son, he gave him the money,
And sent him on his way on a day fine and sunny.

The eldest son stayed, and worked night and day,
And each night he heard his father pray,
'Please God, watch over my youngest son,
Keep him safe and away from harm.'

Now the youngest son was drinking heavily,
And was spending his money very foolishly.
He gambled it all away
And he did bad things every day.

Soon he had nowhere to go and nothing to eat.
His sandals were worn and he had sore feet.
He had to work looking after some pigs, and he ate their food,
And he realised that he had come to no good.

When he could stand it no more, he made up his mind:
I will return to my home where my father was kind.
He would tell his father he would work for his keep,
As long as he would feed him, and find him a place to sleep.

When he was a short way from home,
He saw his father all alone.
And his father looking up saw his son coming near,
And he ran towards him, brushing away a tear.

His son fell before him onto his knees,
'Oh Father,' he begged, 'forgive me, please.
All the money you gave me is gone,
I am not worthy to be called your son.'

His father knelt and put his arms around his thin frame,
'My son, you are home, and I am happy again.
Come we will hurry home and have a feast,
We will roast our very best beast.'

When the eldest son heard of his brother's return,
He felt anger inside him begin to burn.
'Father,' he said, 'I have worked so hard for you.
And now my brother is back, what do you do?

'You treat him just like royalty,
When I am the one who has shown you loyalty.'
So his father put his arms around him, and hugged him tight,
'Yes, my son, what you say is right.

'But we must rejoice this day,
For your brother has been a long time away.
I love you both as much as each other,
And God has returned to you your brother.

'It doesn't matter what it has cost,
For he has returned, the one that was lost.
And if you can forgive your brother too,
God will shed many blessings on you.'

The Tenth Leper

Where Jesus lived, a long time ago,
There were no hospitals where people could go.
Sick people were tended by their families,
Using herbs and potions as their remedies.

If anyone had spots or sores,
They either had to stay indoors
Or, if they went out and about,
They had to cover themselves and shout,
'Unclean, unclean.' And they had to ring a bell,
So that anyone around could tell.
And they had time to get out of the way
At certain times of day.

It was then that the lepers could come out
And collect the food that was left about.
They were suffering from leprosy,
And were a sorry sight to see.

One day, when Jesus was walking about,
He heard the lepers starting to shout.
Everyone ran in their houses to hide,
But Jesus stopped by the lepers' side.

Jesus counted them, and there were ten,
So Jesus stopped and prayed with them.
And on everyone, his hands he laid,
Showing that he was not afraid.

And one by one, they became well.
And they ran off, the people to tell.
But the last leper stayed, and with a cry,
He thanked God, and asked Jesus why.

Why had he saved him from an awful fate,
When he had been in such a dreadful state?
Jesus said, 'God loves everyone,
That is why I did what I have done.

'I healed ten lepers here today,
But nine of them have gone away.
But you, my son, are not like the rest,
You realise you have been blessed.

'Remember to thank God every day
For your good health, and I can say,
My father in heaven will hear your prayer,
And will always keep you in his care.'

Jesus and the Children

Busy, busy, busy, no time to spare.
Jesus was needed everywhere.
There were blind people wanting to see,
Everyone calling to him, 'Heal me, heal me.'

The man who was deaf wanted to hear.
Those who were sick, hoping for a cure.
The dumb who were unable to talk,
The lame were carried to him and he made them walk.

Busy, busy, busy, all the while.
No time to stop and rest awhile.
Then from the crowds, he heard a voice,
Like a whisper spoken above the noise.
A father and mother, and children appeared from the crowd,
And they spoke to Jesus softly, not loud.

One of Jesus' friends, who was standing by,
Glared at the father, and with a sigh
Said, 'Why do you bother Jesus today?
Take your children and go away.
Your children are not ill or dying,
Why are you being so annoying?'

Jesus said to his friend, 'Now wait awhile.'
Then, turning to the parents he gave them a smile
And said, 'What do you want of me?
Your children are well and happy, I can see.'

'Please, Jesus, we have come a long way,
And we would like you to bless our children today.'
Jesus smiled at the children and said, 'Come to me.'
He put his arms around them, and sat them on his knee.

Then he turned to his friends and said,
'Never stop children coming to me.
My father in heaven loves them, you see.
Everyone on earth must be treated the same:
Mothers, fathers, children, the sick and the lame.'

And we can be sure that those children never forgot
That day when they were weary, tired and hot.
That they had met Jesus, and were shown his love,
And he'd given them blessings from his father above.

Zacchaeus the Taxman

The crowds were shouting, 'Jesus is coming to Jericho!'
Everyone wanted to say hello.
But Zacchaeus did not run to meet him.
He did not want to greet him.

Zacchaeus was afraid of the crowd,
And the noise they were making was so loud.
The people did not like Zacchaeus at all,
For he had collected taxes from them all.

In fact, he collected more taxes than he should,
Although he knew that was not good.
And the extra money he kept for himself,
And he hid it in a jar that he kept on the shelf.

He heard the crowds shouting, 'Jesus is here!'
And everyone started to cheer,
I really would like to see him, Zacchaeus thought,
And listen to the words that Jesus taught.

So he had an idea: he would climb up a tree,
And from way up there he would see.
So he chose a tall tree close by,
And he climbed into the branches way up high.

From there he could see Jesus and could hear what he said,
And as he listened, his face turned red.
For the crowd were all begging Jesus to come and eat with them,
But Jesus held up his hand and spoke to them.

'Thank you for your invitations,' he said,
'But I will eat with Zacchaeus instead.'
And Jesus looked up into the tree,
And said, 'Come down here and be with me.'

The people in the crowd were shocked and amazed.
As Zacchaeus climbed down, they gazed and gazed.
Then someone in the crowd shouted,
'He is going to eat with someone who is hated.'

Then everyone stared and was as quiet as a mouse,
As Jesus went with Zacchaeus into his house.
Everyone wondered what was going on,
But they didn't have to wait very long.

For Zacchaeus came out to make an announcement,
And the crowds were stunned with amazement.
'Jesus has made me realise that I have been bad,
And I have made God very sad.

'So I will give back the taxes I stole from you,
And that is not all I will do.
I will sell all that I own, and give half to the poor,
And I promise never to rob anyone ever more.

'Jesus has shown that he loves everyone, even me.
He has changed my life and made me happy.
And the crowds sang and danced the whole night through,
And talked about what God's love could do.'

The Happy Parade

Jesus gathered his friends around him, and told them of his plan,
He said, 'Let us all go down into Jerusalem while we can.
I need to know if the people will be happy to see me,
And I want you all to be with me.'

Jesus knew that not everyone believed he was God's son,
And he knew that his work on earth would soon be done.
So they set out on their journey;
Jesus travelling on the back of a donkey.

The people met them and shouted, 'Hooray!
It is Jesus come to visit us this day!'
And some waved branches from the palm trees,
While others fell worshipping him on their knees.

Others joined hands and started to sing,
'Hooray and hosanna to our king.
This is Jesus, who has been our teacher,
Hooray! This is Jesus, who has been our healer.'

Others took off their cloaks to lay on the ground,
And the donkey walked over them, not making a sound.
Those who hated Jesus yelled at the crowds to stop singing,
But no one took any notice of their yelling.

Everyone was happy, enjoying the parade,
And a band joined in, music was made.
And it would always be remembered as a happy day:
That very first Palm Sunday.

The Important Meal

Jesus and his twelve best friends gathered together for a meal.
The table was laid with bread, lamb and veal.
There was wine in a jug, ready for Jesus to take his place,
And they started saying their before-meal grace.

Instead, Jesus spoke to them saying, 'Tomorrow I have to go away.
So there is something important I have to say.'
His friends stopped their prayers not knowing what to do,
And Jesus said, 'I will miss you.

'But I have to go back to my heavenly father.
Leaving you all, my friends and my mother.
Those who hate me, and do not believe me,
Are going to arrest me and kill me.'

They were horrified at what they had heard,
And for a moment, spoke not a word,
Then they all shouted together, 'We will not let them kill you,
Jesus. Just tell us, what can we do?'

Jesus looked sadly around and said with a frown,
'One of you has already let me down,
And has accepted money to betray me.
He will help them when they come to arrest me.'

They were all very shocked and shouted, 'It was not me!'
Except for one named Judas, and he
Quickly left the room, passing Jesus by.
And Jesus said, 'God bless you' with a sigh.

'Come,' he said, 'let us now eat.'
Then each of the eleven friends took a seat.
Jesus took bread, and for each a piece he broke.
And he looked up to heaven, and these words he spoke:

'This is my body, which will be given up for all men
So that sins may be forgiven.'
Then he took the cup and said, 'This is the cup of my blood. It will be shed for you and all men.
Eat the bread and drink from the cup and
Remember me.'

The Saddest Day

Jesus and his friends went into the garden to pray,
And the soldiers came and arrested him that day.
Judas had done as Jesus had foretold,
And handed Jesus to his enemies of old.

Peter was angry and, without a word,
He tried to injure one of the soldiers with his sword.
But Jesus stopped him and said, 'Put your sword away!'
God has planned all that is to happen this day.'

Jesus was dragged away to court, for them to try him.
Then they took away his clothes and they beat him.
They jeered and said he was not a king,
And they put a crown of thorns on him.

They took a heavy wooden cross and made him carry it,
And when they reached the top of hill, they nailed him on it.
The nails went through his hands and feet,
And he hung on the cross in the boiling heat.

On each side of him two robbers were hanging,
And they heard Jesus to God, his father, praying.
One of the men called to him, 'Save us if you are God's son.'
But the other said, 'We deserve to die for what we have done.

'But this man has done nothing wrong,
And the people will miss him when he is gone.
But no one will miss us when we die today.'
And Jesus heard what he had to say.

'Because you know what you have done is bad,
Do not be unhappy or sad.
Because God is merciful to those who pray,
And you will be in heaven with me today.'

Jesus' mother was standing nearby crying,
And Jesus called to his friend John, and sighing
Said, 'Please look after my mother,
For you have been to me just like a brother.'

Then the sky grew suddenly black everywhere,
And stillness fell upon the air.
And as his friends stood by and cried,
Jesus bowed his head and died.

The Happiest Day

Jesus' friends watched, looking grave,
As Jesus' body in a tomb was laid.
A large stone was placed in front of the tomb,
And they made their way home sadly in the gloom.

Next morning, the sun shone in the sky,
And three women came walking by.
Suddenly the ground began to shake.
They were afraid, and began to quake.

Then everything went very quiet and still,
Even the birds stopped their trill.
One of the women went towards Jesus' grave,
When an angel appeared, which made her afraid.

The stone had been rolled away from the door,
And the sheets that had been around Jesus were on the floor.
But Jesus was nowhere to be seen,
Only an empty tomb where he had been.

'Where has he gone?' the woman cried.
'He has risen from the dead,' the angel replied.
And nearby the three women saw a man,
And they recognised Jesus and to him they ran.

Then Jesus spoke, and told them, 'I am dead no more.
Go and tell my friends to meet me on the sea shore.'
The women ran back to Jerusalem that day,
Telling everyone the good news on the way.

Now the birds sang, and the sky was blue.
The women found Jesus' friends and told them what
   to do.
Some of them went down to Galilee, to the seashore,
And Jesus came to join them once more.

I Don't Believe It

'Thomas, we have good news to tell:
Jesus is alive, and all is well.
We have seen him down by the seashore,
Jesus is not dead, and he will live evermore.'

Thomas just laughed, and shook his head,
'You must be mad,' Thomas said.
'We all saw him die on that sad day,
You must be crazy to talk this way.'

'It is true, it is true,' the others all cried,
'He was there talking and walking by our side.
He lit a fire and cooked fish to eat.
And while we ate, he sat at our feet.'

'It is lies, it is lies; I cannot believe you.'
And the more he spoke the angrier he grew.
'You are wicked; why do you torment me so?
If you don't stop, I will have to go.'

'Calm down,' said Peter, 'and listen to what we say.
We did see Jesus the other day.
He said he would be coming here too,
Especially, just to see you.'

'I want to believe you,' Thomas replied,
'And I will believe you if I see with my eyes.
If I can feel the holes that those awful nails made,
I'll be so happy, and I won't be afraid.'

Suddenly there was sound like the wind rushing by,
And the room filled with light, like the sun in the sky.
Jesus stood before Thomas, showing him a wound,
And Thomas looked at Jesus, and almost swooned.

Jesus laid a soothing hand on Thomas and said,
'Fear not, Thomas, I am with you, I am not dead.'
And Thomas smiled at Jesus with wonder and awe,
'I believe it now I see you, I couldn't before.'

'You believe,' said Jesus, 'because you can see.
But more blessed are those who will come to me
When I am no longer here on earth, but in heaven above.
They will come to me and my father through love.'

The Final Goodbye

With those words, Jesus went from their sight,
And the friends stayed talking all through the night.
They wondered if he would come to them again.
They felt joy and happiness, sorrow and pain.

They did not know when he would finally go,
They only knew they would miss him so.
He had promised they would be in heaven with him one day.
And that he would hear them always, each time they pray.

And soon the time finally came,
When they were on the seashore once again.
Jesus appeared to them just once more,
And walked with them along the seashore.

He said that to his father in heaven he was now returning.
Although the sky was blue, and the sun was shining,
A cloud appeared from nowhere, and wrapped Jesus around.
And so he left them, and disappeared without a sound.

The friends left that place and went their different ways.
They preached to the people and they spent their days
Travelling from place to place, telling the people
Jesus' stories and all of the parables.

And people became Christians and Jesus became known
In countries all over the world, including your own.
And we have read all these stories to you,
Teaching you all the good things that you must do.

We hope you will remember, and when you have children of your own,
Those messages from Jesus, you will pass on.
You will go out into the world and tell everyone,
Just as Jesus told his friends, and we too have done.

Printed in the United Kingdom
by Lightning Source UK Ltd.
126714UK00001B/100/A